Catch Fish With Maps

By The Experts at Fishing Hot Spots

Published by Fishing Hot Spots® Inc., Rhinelander, WI

About the Author:

This book was originally written by Robert Knops, the founder of **Fishing Hot Spots Inc.**, creators and publishers of fishing maps and books for North America. Robert is the author of a number other fishing books, and is a member of the Outdoor Writers Association of America and the Association of Great Lakes Outdoor Writers.

Since it was first published, this book has been revised and updated by the experts at Fishing Hot Spots Inc.

Library of Congress Catalog Card Number:
95-090813

ISBN 0-939314-54-1

Printed in the United States of America

Table of Contents

Foreword

"My view is that the next piece we have to do is integrate all the information into helping anglers make better decisions..... We've got to get to where we help (anglers) make decisions about where they have the best chance for catching fish."

> Louis Chemi,
> Executive Vice President,
> Product Management
> Navico

The quote above was made in early 2009 and is exactly what a good fishing map, like those from Fishing Hot Spots® have been doing for over 30 years, since 1975.

A long known factor to fishing success has been being able to be in the right place at the right time. Fishing maps, as you will learn throughout this book, provide a wealth of information specifically intended to allow anglers to make the best decisions about where to fish. We've all heard the phrase "Location is everything", and this certainly holds true for fishing.

Throughout "How to Catch Fish with Maps," the proper use and interpretation of maps for fishing is thoroughly covered with in-depth explanations and colorful illustrations. By properly knowing how to read a map and translating the information gathered from studying one, you will gain insight into fishing bodies of water and be able to make better choices as to where to devote your fishing time; resulting in greater fishing success.

After reading through this book your understanding of using fishing maps and electronics for planning and on-water use will increase your ability to find and catch more fish. You'll be able to better read any fishing map and "Unfold the Possibilities™" every time you're on the water.

Chapter 1

Fishing Maps:
An Indispensable Angler Tool

There's a lake on the other side of the state that you've been hearing about for years. Word of mouth yields some great stories about superb bass catches. You and your fishing buddy have never been there, but the time of year is right, the weather looks good and you can both take a few days off to travel and cash in on the action. There's no one you know to provide first-hand details, but you and your buddy decide to run over next weekend anyway.

As you're backing your boat down the ramp, you notice the immensity of the lake. "This lake is huge," you mumble. There are 50 trailer rigs in the parking lot but only three boats in sight.

You start working your way down the shoreline. There's no tell-tale characteristics on the shore or in the shallows that would indicate cover. There are no piers or docks. You fan some casts in a number of areas, but don't get a strike.

"This area is dead," your buddy complains. "Let's run across to the other side of the lake." You check depths and profile along the way with your depthfinder. The water is deep, the bottom shaped like a smooth dish pan. There's no discernible structure.

You do find a huge weed flat 100 yards out from the opposite shore, but it's hard to tell where the outside edge is. The weeds just get thinner with no obvious drop-off or bottom change. You work the weeds for four hours and pick up only one 10-inch bass. You and your buddy have better fishing on a pond back home. Now it's 4:00 in the afternoon, and you are really baffled.

Sound familiar? We have all fished blindly like that. It was a complete waste of valuable time! Think of how a detailed map would have put you right on top of the lake's best spots for big bass. Better yet, think about having that map a few days before you left for the lake. You could have...

In the last three decades, maps made for anglers have become synonymous with catching fish. You no longer have to spend time learning a body of water the way the old-timers did: by sheer expense of time and effort. Expert fishermen spent 10 to 20 seasons trying to discover the peculiarities of one lake so they could eventually catch fish consistently. Today, for less than the price of a good crankbait, you can obtain a professionally made, highly accurate, waterproof and tearproof picture of the underwater world you fish. Map companies learned the lake for you. Now all you do is follow their maps and catch fish.

Maps, particularly those designed for fishermen, present a great deal of information. First, maps are oriented directionally. They have

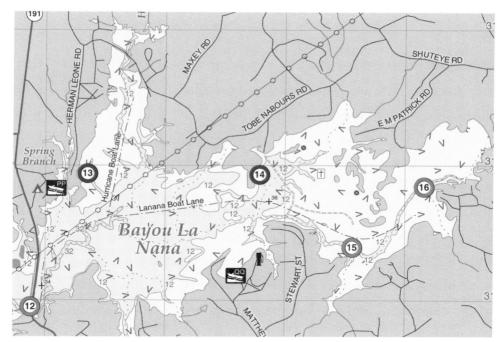

Man Made Reservoirs *are characterized by submerged features that fish relate to. These would include underwater roadbeds, cemeteries, and flooded timber.*

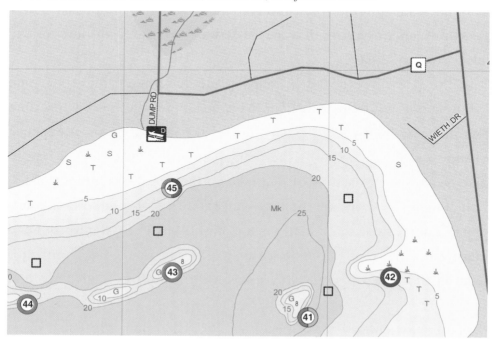

Natural Lakes *(with fish habitat such as humps, various bottom compositions and different weed types)*

4

a compass rose or north arrow showing both true and magnetic north. You can turn your map so that it faces the same direction the lake faces. Positioning a map correctly helps you catch fish. You can relate lake features to predict the effects of sunlight and wind direction, as well as simplify navigation.

All maps are drawn proportionally or scaled. It is not feasible to provide a life-size drawing, so a selected length on the map represents an actual distance on the lake. Each map uses its own scale because sizes of mapped areas vary. Anglers can determine distance from one "hot spot" to another using the map's scale.

As an overall reference, a good fishing map provides latitude and longitude information and Global Positioning System (GPS) coordinates. These two features assist in consistently knowing where you are, where you want to go and provide a way to always find or return to an exact location.

Maps have limited space, so symbols represent a variety of features. The map legend defines those symbols. A few examples of map symbols include creek channels, weeds, man-made fish attractors, boat landings, flooded timber, and navigation hazards.

A significant feature on today's fishing maps

is depth measurement or contour lines. Fish rarely inhabit the surface. They spend most of their lives well below the surface. Reading and understanding contour lines are the two most important skills in finding fish.

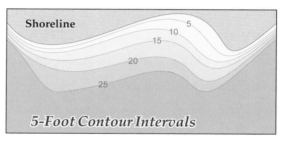

5-Foot Contour Intervals

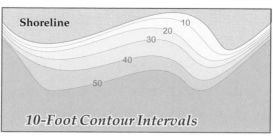

10-Foot Contour Intervals

Depending on the size and scale of the map, contour lines can represent 2-foot intervals up to 40-foot intervals. A series of closely spaced contour lines represent a sharp drop-off, while widely spaced lines represent a gradual slope. Contours will be discussed in greater detail later.

Fishing maps show locations fish frequent. "Structure" is the term most frequently used to describe these places.

Fish relate closely to boat docks, fallen trees, underwater islands, weedbeds, and anything unusual to the normal underwater scene. Maps identify these potential fish-catching sites.

Contour or hydrographic maps show edges. An edge is the end of some type of structure or cover, such as a weedline, brushline or the borders of an old creek channel. Edges attract gamefish because edges are major feeding areas. Knowing where edges exist will put you in direct contact with fish.

Fishermen often use the term "breakline" to describe a distinct increase in depth. Breaklines can be located by studying maps. The term is also used to denote areas where there are definite changes in other characteristics such as water clarity, temperature and oxygen content.

Transition zones are found where bottom changes from one material to another. An example of a transition would be a tapering sand flat ending in a bottom of solid rock. Fish relate closely to the zone where the materials change. Carefully reading a map will help you find these breaklines and transition zones in the bodies of water you fish.

Using a map of a lake or reservoir will prevent you from fishing water where there are no fish. You can concentrate your efforts on the most productive sections in the lake. When you pick up some allegedly hot tip about a certain body of water, studying a map will help you confirm or deny the information.

Once you become familiar with what a map can do to improve your fishing, you will not want to venture out on a lake without one. A map is just as important to catching fish as a depthfinder or even a tackle box full of lures.

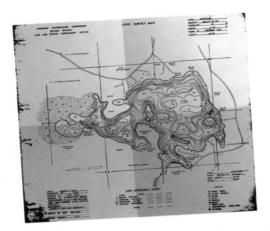

Chapter 2
A Very Brief History of Mapping

The history of the typical inland lake map goes back more than a century. The federal government, state governments and private utilities developed maps for commerce, military intelligence, fishery management and flood control. These early maps showed erratic depths, inconsistent contour lines, and often inaccurate depictions of the lake's shape.

Ocean maps, or charts as they are called, date back centuries. The charts of this country's major river systems were first authorized by Congress in 1816. By 1818, the U.S. Topographic Corps of Engineers mapped the Ohio and lower Mississippi Rivers. By 1837, Lt. Robert E. Lee (who would later become famous in the War Between the States) mapped and blasted a navigation channel on the upper Mississippi

River from Keokuk, Iowa, north.

During the 19th century the United States Army Corps of Engineers began surveying the Great Lakes. The Corps drawn charts are now known as National Oceanic and Atmospheric Administration (NOAA) charts.

NOAA charts clearly define depths for the Great Lakes and connecting waters. Although originally made for commercial navigators, fishermen quickly realized the value of these charts and began using them to find fish.

Prior to electronic sounding, depth measurements were obtained by lowering a marked or knotted line to the bottom. Surveyors positioned each reading using a process known as transecting--which created a series of regular and intersecting intervals that crisscrossed the water. Map making in the early days was labor intensive and time consuming.

During the 20th century, America began impounding rivers and streams to create huge reservoirs and flowages. Topographical maps from the United States Geological Survey (U.S.G.S.) done prior to flooding an area became the basis for many lake maps once the reservoirs were filled.

While these maps depict considerable detail, they show reservoir contour lines as land elevations prior to impoundment but not as water depths. Anglers had to mentally convert elevations to depth.

Translating topographical land maps into underwater contour maps (hydrographic) also poses another problem. Printed maps are based on a single water level, meaning they show a reservoir at specified lake or pool elevation. If water levels rise due to spring runoff, or drop during a drought, maps do not compensate for the variation. An impoundment map must identify an existing or normal pool level as its basis, so anglers can then project possible depth changes based on higher or lower water levels.

Highly detailed pre-impoundment land surveys by the Army Corps of Engineers were also done. These maps not only showed contours but also depicted buildings, roadbeds, railroad grades and fence lines, as well as areas where flooded timber would be left standing.

The fishing map itself has a very short history. Anglers did not begin using fishing maps until the early 1960's--coincidental with the introduction of electronic depthfinders. Suddenly, a whole new world of electronic and cartographic information changed fishing into a science. Once anglers could coordinate their fishing map with depthfinder data, they could mark their map accordingly. The fishing map was born.

There are five general types of maps available to anglers--arranged here in increasing order of fishing information.

1. Overview maps: These include state atlases, county and regional maps that locate lakes and streams as well as major road systems. Although these maps are useful for determining how to get to the lake, water detail is lacking. *(See image 1, pg. 14)*

2. U. S. G. S. Quadrangle Maps: These maps are commonly referred to as "quads" or "topos." They show land contours (topography), roads, towns, plus various land and water features. The large-scale 7 1/2 minute series quads are available for nearly the entire country and have a standardized scale of 1 inch equals 2,000 feet. *(See image 2, pg. 14)*

Even though many of these maps are dated, detail for fishermen is adequate. They show some boat landings shown as well as stream bridge crossings, natural landmarks and general topography. However, quads often do not furnish detailed lake contour/depth information.

3. Navigation Charts: Made only for large, commercially navigable rivers, the Great Lakes and saltwater, these charts are accurate, but costly. Navigation charts, as the name implies, show dredged channels, buoys, piers, reefs, shoals, and hazards in excellent detail to assure safe boating. *(See image 3, pg. 15)*

4. Lake or River Maps: Maps of this type concentrate on water depths and sub-surface structures. Lake maps show little of the surrounding area and road information. They furnish little fishing data. Most of these maps were made many years ago and are often inaccurate. *(See image 4, pg. 15)*

5. Fishing Maps: Quality fishing maps feature an accurate contour/depth map of a lake or river, but also offer first-rate fishing and navigation information. Created specifically for anglers, these maps show water features essential for locating fish such as weedbeds, brush piles, old creek/river channels, flooded timber and submerged roadbeds. Fishing maps are accurately drawn to scale and include approach roads to boat landings, marinas and parks.

Today's fishing map makers, such as Fishing Hot Spots, use the latest computer and location-based technology to create maps that are accurate, colorful and easy-to-read. They produce a tackle-box-handy fishing map that combines excellent cartography with angling information. Quality fishing maps provide great detail of the surface and underwater world of fish. Fishermen can quickly learn a lake by using and understanding the wealth of information available from a good fishing map. *(See image 5, pg. 16)*

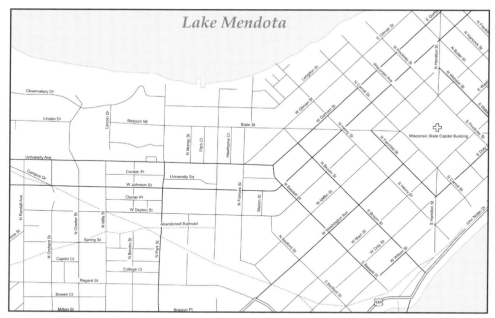

1. Overview Map

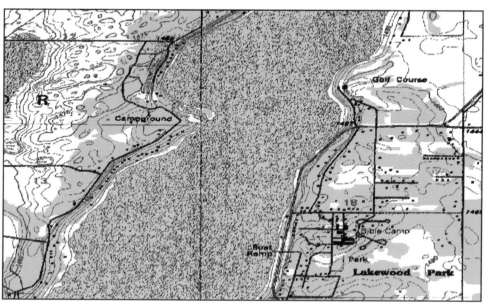

2. U.S.G.S. Quadrangle Map

14

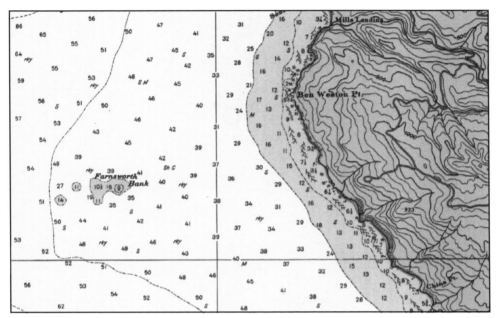

3. Navigation Chart

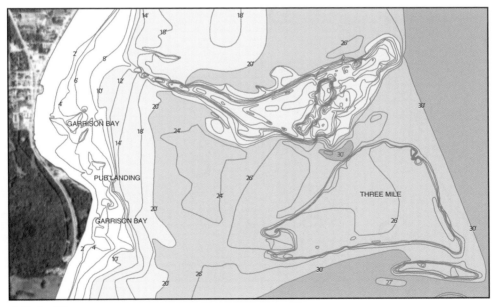

4. Lake Map

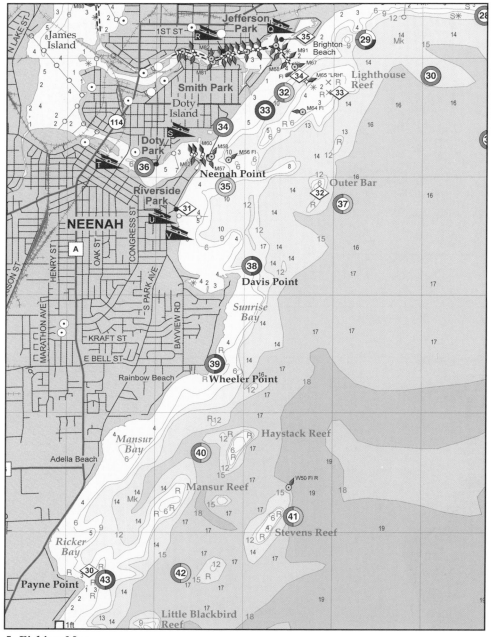

5. Fishing Map

16

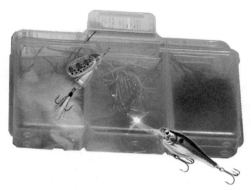

Chapter 3
Planning A Fishing Trip

I t is improbable that someone would take an extended trip to an unfamiliar destination without a map. It would certainly be a waste of time, money and effort. Worse yet, the person runs the risk of becoming lost. Yet lots of fishermen, including the two whose story introduced this book, fish strange waters without a map.

As a highway map shows you precisely how to arrive at a desired destination, lake maps show you probable fish-catching spots and how to get to each one.

But a fishing map tells you many important things long before you arrive at the lake. Maps mark marinas and boat launch areas. You can pick the one that is most conveniently located to your route, the one closest to the areas you want to fish, or the one located in the protection of a sheltered harbor.

A map helps you determine what kind of fishing gear you need. If, for example, the map shows extended ranges of flooded timber, you should bring a medium-to-heavy action rod and a reel spooled with tough fishing line. It would be tragic if you hooked a record bass only to have it break off in submerged tree limbs because you spooled 8-pound test line rather than 20-pound test.

A map also designates depths. If you decide to fish a reservoir like the famous Lake Fork in Texas, a map of the diverse lake suggests you may have to fish a variety of depths before you locate largemouth. That means your tackle box should have light-weight baits designed to work the surface and relative shallows. If you do not find fish in the upper levels of the lake, you will have to cast deeper--off the deep points and perhaps even drop down to the old creek channels. That means heavy artificials like 3/4-ounce jigs, lead slabs, and Texas-rigged worms.

On the other hand, if you are going to fish Florida's Lake Okeechobee which is mostly shallow water with slowly tapering drop-offs, you will stock your tackle box with crankbaits, light-weight jigs, and unweighted plastic lizards, centipedes, and short worms. An abundance of vegetation symbols on the map means weedless spoons, spinnerbaits, and unweighted worms.

Careful attention to a map before going on the water allows an angler to select proper gear. The prepared angler spends their time on the water catching fish, not off the water hunting for a proper rod and reel, or combing tackle shops looking for the right baits.

Do not assume the casual recreational angler is the only one who analyzes a map before fishing. Before making a cast, expert fishermen and seasoned tournament pros study lake maps with the intensity of an Ivy League scholar.

Why do the experts study maps before they hit the water? To develop a plan. They fish more efficiently and effectively by using a map to evaluate a lake and then develop a strategy based on such factors as the target species, type of water, and time of year. By knowing where you are going to fish before leaving the boat landing, you go directly to the spots with the highest fish-holding potential, you don't have to race around randomly looking for a good place to fish.

The most important benefit of using maps to pre-plan is eliminating unproductive water. By combining basic knowledge of fish with information from a map, successful anglers arrive at the lake prepared, catch more fish, and have more fun.

Pre-planning with maps has obvious benefits when venturing to new water, but it also can improve your catch on familiar waters. Perhaps your once-secret honey hole is now the most popular spot on the lake. Many times productive spots on a favorite lake just stop producing fish. Maybe a sunken brush pile finally deteriorated and rotted away, or a terrific weed edge is no longer evident, or perhaps water levels or clarity have changed and altered fish patterns. Whatever the reason, you must find some new spots. Using a good fishing map will certainly help. By studying a map, you can quickly locate spots similar to those where you have consistently caught fish.

The following experience illustrates the value of studying maps before getting on the water. The relatively small amount of time spent preparing will pay back big dividends with more fish in the boat.

Bob Kline is one the country's best muskie fishermen. Huge mounted muskies line the walls of Kline's recreation room. He has spent his life studying and catching muskellunge.

Some years back, Bob accepted a challenge. Could he fish a lake he had never before seen, in a part of the country he had never fished, and catch a 30-inch or longer muskie within three days? If you are a gambler, that's not a bet you would take. Muskies, sometimes referred to as the fish of 10,000 casts, are not easy to catch, much less from a lake you do not know.

The first thing Kline did in preparing for the challenge was obtain a contour map of the selected lake. He highlighted a sequence of features--rock reefs, sharply shaped points jutting into the lake, underwater humps and irregularly shaped shorelines on the map. Those features near exceptionally deep water received, top priority consideration.

Before making a cast, Bob motored over each one of his selected areas. He kept one eye on his depthfinder and the other on the contour map. When the depthfinder showed a sudden change in the structure or weed growth in the area, he marked his map.

With his own marked map, he then systematically cast each pre-determined spot. It took nearly two days for Kline to work the lake, but at 6:00 p.m. on the second day he boated a muskie that weighed 27 pounds and measured 47 inches in length. He caught the fish off one of his marked underwater humps.

Bob Kline proved that careful analysis of a map, coupled with knowledge and persistence, catches fish. "I would never have attempted a stunt like that without a map," Kline stated. Even the experts find maps indispensable. That is one reason they are expert anglers.

Chapter 4
The World of Fish

Fish have three basic urges. First, each species requires acceptable habitat - a safe territory with appropriate light, temperature and dissolved oxygen content. Secondly, fish need a ready supply of food. And third, fish must have the opportunity to reproduce and perpetuate the species. As an angler comes to understand the habits and behavior of his quarry, he can more easily locate fish and catch them.

Environment and instinct dictate a fish's behavior patterns. The cold-blooded fish seeks a comfort zone, preferring to locate in a temperature layer that also provides safety. For example, the bronze mottled and barred coloration of smallmouth bass blends well with underwater rock bars and shelves. Rocks provide these bass with camouflage (safety). Rocks are also home to one of the smallmouth's favorite foods, the crayfish. Not all rocky areas in a lake will hold smallies, however, a savvy smallmouth angler looks at a fishing map and finds underwater rocks, then fishes only those areas suitable for bass. Smallmouth may find rocks in the shallows too warm and bright, and rocks in super-deep water devoid of oxygen. A map's contour lines bracket rock areas in between these two extremes--the best places to fish.

Fish must eat regularly. Once a fisherman knows the basic diet of the species he seeks, he can locate areas where that food supply exists. Muskellunge prefer suckers in their diet, particularly the common white sucker. These suckers prefer flowing water.

Since fishing maps designate creek inlets, the well-prepared muskie angler will look at a map and find shallow bays fed by creeks or small rivers. These areas are likely to attract suckers, and therefore, muskie. Casting brownish-gray sucker-pattern plugs that mimic the forage will increase his chances for success. A muskie outing based on mapped information is much

Water Temperature Perferred by Species

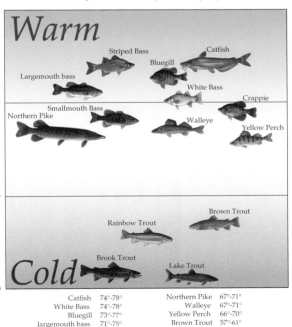

Catfish	74°-78°	Northern Pike	67°-71°
White Bass	74°-78°	Walleye	67°-71°
Bluegill	73°-77°	Yellow Perch	66°-70°
largemouth bass	71°-75°	Brown Trout	57°-61°
Striped bass	70°-74°	Rainbow Trout	56°-62°
Crappie	69°-73°	Brook Trout	52°-56°
Smallmouth bass	68°-72°	Lake Trout	50°-52°

more productive than random searches.

Every species of fish has a specific set of criteria for carrying out its reproductive chores. A popular fish all over the country, the white bass, spawns when water reaches 58 degrees. Schools of whites (also called sand bass in some parts of the country) seek gravel bottoms in 6 to 7 feet of fairly clear water with either a measurable current or significant wind action to successfully reproduce. If you fish for white bass in any of the nation's large reservoirs, you will want to fish when the water temperature and conditions are right.

Springtime white bass anglers should look for shallow contours-- but which ones? A map will tell you. Reservoirs are fed by a series of rivers and creeks, each entering the main body of water from its own cove. Most of these coves have water shallow enough for white bass to spawn. Since these bass want flowing or wind-swept water, if you find creek arms with significant flow or areas wide enough to be affected by wind, the fish will likely be there, not in small wind-protected or inlet-free coves.

Finding fish is not always as simple as relating your search to comfort, food supply and spawning requirements. There are several other factors that play important roles in the process. If, for example, you know that largemouth bass are most comfortable and active in water at 75 degrees, that does not suggest that you will catch largemouth everywhere you find water that temperature. You have to target water

Figures 4.1 & 4.2 Since light penetrates to greater depths in clear water *(above)* fish tend to suspend deeper than they normally would if the water was murky or stained *(below).*

that provides bass with other features. If one of those areas is also 75 degrees, you stand a good chance of finding Mr. Bucketmouth.

Structure is more bassy than open water. Why? Structure provides bass with protective cover. Structure leads bass to food. Structure may provide shade from the rays of the sun. Open water affords none of these opportunities for bass. What is the best way to find structure? Look at your fishing map. The legend has symbols which represent various types of structure. Check all these marked areas and you are most likely to find largemouth bass.

Fish relate to many underwater characteristics. Maps identify these features. California's Lake Sonoma is a typical, structure-rich reservoir. Sonoma has off-shore weedbeds which at certain times are red-hot bass fishing spots, but, bass are not always in the weeds. They find plenty of cover and food scattered among the lake's flooded timber. Top quality fishing maps highlight flooded timber and lead you to bass when weeds are not productive.

Docks and piers are good examples of fish-holding structure. Sharp drop-offs, weed edges, turns in a creek channel, intersections of two creek channels, submerged points, off-shore humps, mud flats, rock reefs, brush piles, man-made fish attractors, abrupt changes in bottom composition, and a myriad of similar underwater features are magnets for fish. Fishing maps identify these features. The more you study a map, the more fish you will have the opportunity to meet on the end of your line.

Light is another factor in determining fish location. Generally, fish avoid bright light. Light penetrates clear water much more intensely than cloudy water. Fish tend to frequent deeper water in gin-clear lakes compared to lakes with water the clarity of coffee mixed with cream (see *Figures 4.1 & 4.2*).

Fish usually prefer shade to unshaded areas. They can avoid light in two general ways, either by moving to deeper water where light penetration is reduced, or by moving into the shade of an overhanging object such as a dock, tree or boathouse. Fish often avoid bright light by burying themselves at the base of thick weed growth like coontail, milfoil or hydrilla.

Maps help anglers take advantage of a fish's tendency to seek cover and shade. Since maps have a directional arrow (pointing north), fishermen can predict the shaded sides of the entire lake and shaded areas of specific structure. You can determine, just by looking at a map, if an underwater tapering point off the northeast side of an island will be sunny or shady at 3:15 p.m.

A fish's position on the food chain is significant in how it relates to cover. Panfish like crappie and bream seek cover much more readily than northern pike, muskellunge and huge bass. Panfish are lower on the freshwater food chain, while the pike family is at the top. Since muskellunge have been known to attack anything that moves, this opportunistic fish is found in many different locations--from shorelines looking for ducklings to deep offshore walleye reefs. Crappie feed on small minnows and insects and do not stray too far from these important foods. Crappie will school near minnow-holding structure like weedbeds, brush piles, fallen trees, and shoreline riprap and docks.

Study a fishing map to find areas likely to hold the preferred food of the species you seek. You will not fish randomly or "blind" when you coordinate your position and lure (or bait) presentation with a fishing map.

Chapter 5
Finding Fish on a Map

F ish spend most of their time in sanctuaries--holed up where they are safe and comfortable (adequate oxygen and acceptable temperature). Except in extreme cases, fish sanctuaries are the deepest pockets in a defined area that includes access to food. A fish's instinctive behavior limits the boundaries of its territory.

One theory of fish behavior contends all species of fish move from their sanctuaries to areas where they actively feed. Hunger triggers movement. When their stomachs are full, they return to their sanctuaries.

Another theory maintains that weather and light activate fish movement. Low pressure storm fronts stimulate fish to move and feed. When the front passes and the weather clears, fish are less

Light   *and **weather***   *influence **feeding***

active and are found tight to cover. Regardless of what causes fish movement, expect them to move regularly within a set territory.

Another principle of fish behavior is all movement takes place along defined routes. Fish orient themselves with certain features of their underwater environment and travel set pathways between feeding areas and holding areas.

While it is possible to catch fish suspended over deep water, or when they move into deep, structureless water, your chances of catching them are much greater as they migrate or feed in the shallows.

A map will help you find all three important fish zones: sanctuaries, travel routes, and feeding areas. The map search process should begin by first identifying likely feeding areas.

Many types of fish--crappie, largemouth bass, smallmouth bass, white bass, striped bass, hybrid striped bass, walleye, northern pike, muskie, large trout to cite a few--feed on minnows or forage fish. Schools of minnows thrive in warm water. If you are fishing for minnow feeders, start at the shoreline where the water will be warm. While you are going over the shoreline on your map, find areas that will hold schools of minnows--places with vegetation, or brush piles, or where artificial fish attractors have been secured.

The shore areas you identified will only be visited regularly by gamefish if they have easy access to the spot and a definite and protected route to get there. Here is where a fishing map becomes an invaluable tool.

Gamefish often prefer relatively deep water near their feeding grounds. Look at each possible shoreline foraging area you found and check the surroundings for much deeper water. If you find none, chances are the spot will be unproductive. The opposite is also true, however. If you find a sharp drop-off near a shoreline brush pile, fish will be there dining on minnows.

Figure 5.1 illustrates a shoreline area with shallow (warm) water, but weeds, wood and other forms of cover are lacking. The off-shore area has a slow gradual drop with no discernible deep hole or evidence of structure to create a sanctuary. This area offers little to attract fish and should not be your first choice fishing spot.

Figure 5.2 shows a weedbed with lily pads and other weeds on a 5-foot flat--a natural for minnows. At the edge of the flat the water drops sharply to 20 feet, and just beyond the 20-foot level is a hole that is 33 feet deep. Fish often move from shallow feeding areas and suspend nearby over deep water. They can easily move from the deep water to the weed and pad growth. It is a short swim to the minnow haven where they will feed.

You found two shallow areas. One is a hot spot; the other is not. The information on your fishing map tells you to concentrate on one and avoid the other.

You have also found a secondary place to catch fish by map reading. If you fish the weeds and pads and wind up empty, cast all along the

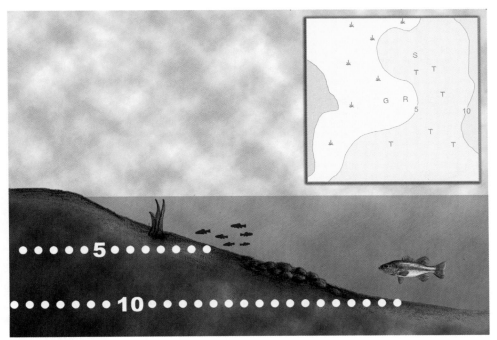

Figure 5.1

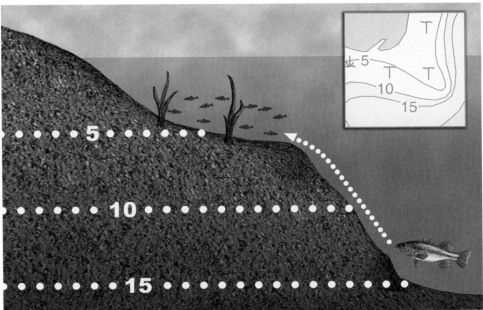

Figure 5.2 *Gamefish are likely to hold in areas that offer easy access to their feeding grounds*

***Figure* 5.3** *Fish will hold at lower depths during high light periods*

***Figure* 5.4** *Fish will hold closer to the surface during low light periods*

36

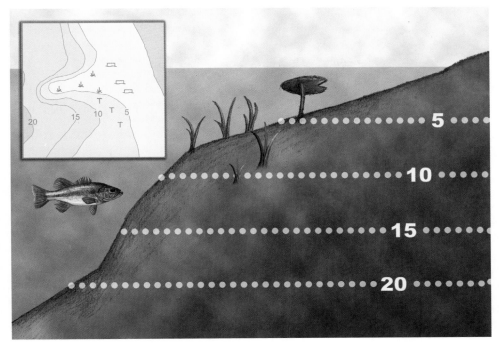

Figure 5.5

route connecting their feeding area and deep water. You will need jigs and deep-diving plugs to probe the area.

What is the best way to fish their regular route? Will the fish be heading to the shore or back to their holding area? In summer, when fish metabolic rates are highest, they need to make numerous forays to feeding territories. The cooler the water, the less often they feed.

For sake of discussion, let's assume you find no fish in the shallows. Your next step is to position yourself over deeper water along the drop-off. Before you make a cast, look at the amount and direction of light. Next determine wind direction. If you find sunlight beaming down from a high sky--as it would from 10:00 am to 3:00 pm--fish the deepest end of the break. Remember fish tend to avoid light. If the sun is low and does not illuminate the water substantially, let the wind direction determine where you will fish.

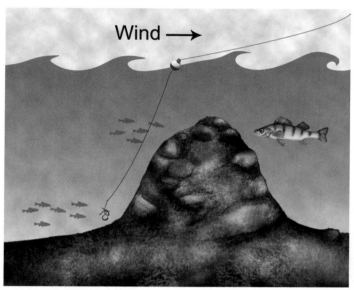

Wind ⟶

Wind on the surface of the water moves baitfish and other foods. Predators wait at an ambush point (in the diagram to the left, on the leeward side of the hump) for food to blow into their range. You want to cast your bait into the wind and retrieve it in the direction of the water flow. This presentation best simulates actual fish feeding conditions.

Lastly, you can fish the deep water for suspended fish if the pads, weeds, and routes in between do not produce. Since suspended fish can be anywhere between the bottom and surface, a depthfinder is essential for determining the proper depth to present your bait.

A map with a north arrow or compass rose will assist you in making choices where to fish. If the wind is blowing a gale, some windswept areas will be unsafe. A map will tell you which coves will be calm and fishable and which will not. A map can also be used to find the safest possible route to calm waters. You may also choose not to fish one body of water because a south wind, for example, churns it to an unfishable froth. Another lake that is narrow and runs from east to west would be a much less windy choice.

Top-of-the-line fishing maps, such as those produced by Fishing Hot

Spots, include a section of proven tips and techniques to enhance your fishing. Angling experts put together a list of hot baits and techniques that are helpful in getting you started on the lake or reservoir. These maps put you a quantum leap ahead of the user of a plain contour map.

Chapter 6

GPS Mapping, your eyes underwater

D epthfinders have become an integral part of every angler's tools over the past decade or so. Continued price decreases, better quality and a more comprehensive understanding of how to use them for fishing has made them standard equipment in virtually every boat.

The term depthfinder refers to a device utilizing sonar. Sonar emits high frequency sound waves that are inaudible to fish and humans. These impulses strike an object and reflect back to a receiver. The receiver measures the time it took for the impulses to return and continually calculates the distance between it and the object. Screens, graphs, or calibrated flashes display distance.

The depthfinder has two parts, a main unit and a transducer. The electrical power to operate the sonar comes from either your boat's 12-volt system or a self-contained battery source. When you turn the depthfinder on, it begins sending impulses through the transducer. The transducer receives the echo signal and sends it to the main processing unit. There the angler reads the information on the display.

There are several different types of depthfinders available, primarily distinguished by how the sonar information is displayed. The basic types are: Flasher, Liquid Crystal Display (LCD), Digital and Cathode Ray Tube (CRT). LCD's have become the most commonly used by today's anglers and are available in numerous styles and price ranges. Depthfinder technology for sportfishermen has come a long way since its inception just a few decades ago. Newly discovered technologies are further enhancing depthfinder science.

The data you obtain from a depthfinder screen, in part, includes: bottom composition, bottom terrain, depth, structure type and configuration, presence of fish, size of fish, and submerged weeds and wood. With the bank of information a depthfinder furnishes, savvy anglers can create a complete representation of the fish's world--a picture that will allow them to catch more fish.

A depthfinder display requires interpretation by the angler. For example, a good depthfinder depicts not only the bottom of a lake, but bottom composition as well. You can tell bottom composition by reading the base line on screen or observing the width of the flash.

To illustrate how this reading works, imagine you are blindfolded and throwing a tennis ball against three surfaces, a brick wall, a mattress, and a swimming pool. A friend stands next to you with a catcher's mitt to catch the ball. When a thrown ball smacks loudly into the glove, you would know it reflected off the brick surface. If the ball hit with a dull thud, you would know it hit a softer surface, the mattress. When the ball did not return, you'd realize it was absorbed by the water.

The depthfinder works the same way. If the screen shows a wide line, the bottom material is hard, such as sand, gravel or rock. When you read a thinner line, the transducer signal echoed off a soft bottom. No signal or a faint return indicates a marsh or bog of inestimable depth.

Gamefish, weedbeds, fish attractors, submerged timber, schools of forage fish, and all other underwater objects show on a depthfinder. It is the angler's job to view the display and interpret the information. Although a depthfinder manual will help you start this interpretive process, nothing beats first hand, on-the-water experience.

Particular depthfinders vary greatly from basic units to extremely sophisticated technical models. Prices vary accordingly. What features should you look for in a depthfinder?

Readability is first on the list. Anglers need to see depthfinder information at a glance. Over the years manufacturers have been working to increase readability. Recent improvements include larger, sunlight readable displays and the option of full-color presentations of submerged features.

Automation is another valuable feature. You came to the lake to fish, not to fool with complicated electronic gadgetry. For ease of operation, most depthfinders automatically adjust to whatever fishing conditions exist. Many, however, have manual override systems allowing each angler to use customized settings.

A depthfinder must have sufficient output power to read at high speeds. Low wattage finders only read at rest or slow speeds. It is advisable to spend a bit more for a higher powered unit than to scrimp on a less expensive model.

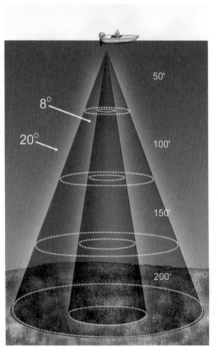

Look for a depthfinder that has a cone angle suited for the type of waters you fish. Cone angle works like this. The impulses emitted from a unit travel from the transducer. Instead of traveling in one straight line, the signals spread out into a series of narrow, medium or wide concentric circles. Common cone angles range from 8 degrees (narrow) to around 60 degrees (wide). The wider the cone angle, the broader the coverage and the less precise the screen readout. Conversely, the narrower the cone angle, the tighter the coverage and the more precise the reading. Most freshwater anglers find a medium cone angle (in the 20-degree range) right for the waters they fish and for locating a mapped hot spot.

Some manufacturers now market depthfinders that have multiple cone angle capabilities. You can manually shift from a narrow cone angle to a wide cone angle with the push of a button. One company even sells a finder that presents a dual screen where you see two cone angles simultaneously. Others offer a variety of interchangeable transducers so you can select the particular cone angle you prefer. Spend some time looking at features to make sure you buy a unit that is right for you.

Other desirable features of a depthfinder include zoom and freeze framing. At times you will want to take a closer look at a screen. Hit the stop button and the image locks on-screen for extended examination. Zooming allows the operator to enlarge a given area to enhance details.

Some depthfinders include a surface temperature gauge and others make temperature measurement an optional accessory. Any angler will appreciate knowing water temperature (see chapter 4 for the effect of temperatures on fish behavior).

If you like bells and whistles, you can get a depthfinder that beeps every time it identifies a fish (the beeper has a shutoff switch for those times you prefer the sounds of nature).

While depthfinders are great fishing tools, they become doubly useful when coordinated with fishing maps. What are some of the ways a depthfinder enhances a fishing map?

1. Knowing a precise location

If you are unsure about your correct position, check the fishing map by reading the closest contour (depth) line. If your depthfinder agrees with your map, you have at least isolated the general location.

2. Updating your fishing map

Navigating with a fishing map and a depthfinder tells the angler if his map is correct. Also, if you happen to find an unmapped fishing spot (mid-lake hump, abrupt underwater point, breakline or similar honey hole) with your depthfinder, you can draw in the spot on your map.

3. Finding specific locations and structures

Although a fishing map presents many details on finding areas to fish, a depthfinder is necessary to confirm that exact location. You may want to crisscross a potential fish bonanza a few times with the depthfinder to determine the correct profile of the mapped structure.

4. Visualizing a 3-D image

Most depthfinders show a one or two-dimensional image. On an LCD, for example, you see a bottom line, surface line and objects located between. That is enough data for an angler to project his own mental view of the subsurface environment.

5. Staying on edges with fish

Weed edges and breaklines are outstanding places to catch fish. Both appear on fishing maps, but an angler must have a depthfinder to stay on top of them. Both lines are highly irregular. If you are drift fishing or using an electric motor, you've got to keep one eye on the depthfinder screen to make sure you are in casting range of these edges.

6. Estimating distance

If you know the speed at which you are traveling, distance is easy to calculate. Some depthfinders even display speed and distance traveled on screen.

7. Locating fish

Maps made specifically for fishermen, such as Fishing Hot Spots maps, identify plenty of information relative to the location of fish. When you attempt to fish one of these particular zones, a depthfinder will often times tell you whether fish are present. Motor on to the next predetermined area when you find no fish on the screen. Depthfinders will save you thousands of casts over time.

Chapter 7
Visualization of the Fish's World

Now that you have coordinated the stream of data from your depthfinder with a fishing map, you will take the next step and develop the ability to visualize. The process takes patience and practice. Once you learn to visualize, however, you will catch fish like a professional.

Brian Vaughn, bass tournament angler, puts it this way, "Before I knew about visualization, fishing was a hit-and-miss proposition. Once I learned to visualize underwater structure and mentally see where bass locate, I started catching significantly more fish with the consistency that tournaments demand."

How does visualization work and why is learning the technique so important to today's angler? Visualization is the ability to form a mental picture of something that is beyond your sight.

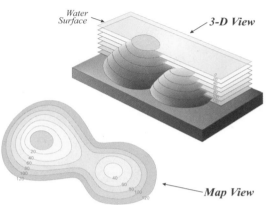

Since you can not see beneath the surface of the water very far, you have to create in your mind's eye what drop-offs, weed edges, rock reefs, inside turns, contours and creek channels look like. Then you mentally add where fish are likely to be or where your depthfinder shows them.

To visualize, you have to translate the two-dimensional flat fishing map into a multi-dimensional picture. Even the 3-D image you see on some depthfinder screens is not as complete as a mental visualization.

To start you on the road to visualization, try the following exercise. Picture a trout stream or smallmouth bass creek that cuts its way through the floor of a valley. Position yourself fishing in the center of the valley. The east bank of the stream runs along the base of a steep cliff. The west shore borders a flat about 25 yards wide then rises into a rolling hill. Stop casting for a minute and look around. Familiarize yourself with the base of the valley and then the hillsides. Now place an imaginary dam at the lower end of the stream. Your valley is now filled with water.

No longer are the fish confined to the small stream. They can swim anywhere they want within your newly created reservoir. Try to picture the kinds of places fish would locate. Would smallmouth prefer the side of the steep cliff where that old tree remains? Would

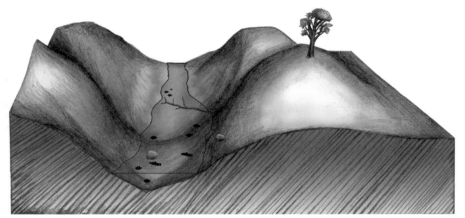

Figure 7.1 *A view of a stream running through a valley. The fish are confined to the stream bed.*

Figure 7.2 *A view of a stream that has been damned resulting in a flooded valley. As a result, the fish are free to occupy structures that were once above water.*

largemouth bass and walleye seek sanctuary along the edges of the old stream channel? Would trout seek the cold water at the base of the dam? Might a school of crappie suspend off the tall grass at the top of the west hill? Would a muskie or northern pike suspend near the bream? If you stocked striped bass would they roam the center of the reservoir looking for schools of shad?

All these images are real. Your newly flooded valley is exactly what a natural lake or impounded reservoir looks like underwater. You should picture every body of water you fish in the same way--not as a flat surface, but as a three-dimensional, real-life world with fish locating at strategic spots.

Now that you have an initial visualization of an entire body of water, zero in on one particular structure. To illustrate, refer to the map of Bass Lake and the submerged island or hump. The map shows that the top of the hump is 3 feet below the surface and rises 17 feet off the bottom.

Before you make a cast to the hump, picture an oblong hill 17 feet high. Next, use the map's scale and measure the base of the hump. The base is roughly 375 feet long by 175 feet wide. Do not forget to cut the indentation into the hump on the southeast side.

With a picture of a 375' x 175' x 17' oblong structure firmly implanted in your mind, next estimate where the most likely fish hang-outs will be. If you guessed the cut on the southeast slope, you are probably right. That cut has all the qualities of a prime fishing spot. It offers a deep-water holding area and is near a shallow feeding zone--the point off the island to the northeast and the large weedy bay to the east.

If this hump were in much deeper water, you could run your boat and depthfinder over the top to confirm your suspicions about fish location. Since the hump rises so close to the surface, a motor boat going over the top might spook fish and ruin your chances.

If you have trouble picturing all that information in your mind, try an alternate approach. Before you go fishing, put a lake map on your kitchen table and draw a sketch of the hump or other structure on a piece of paper. Start with the top of the hump and then extend lines downward off the top to create a three-dimensional effect. Sometimes all it takes to start visualizing is that first sketch. From then on the process will be second nature to you.

Are you ready to make a cast to your visualized hump? Your only choice now is where to position the boat and retrieve your cast? If walleye or bass use the hump, position the boat southeast of the hump, throw a jig on top, and bounce it down the southeast side into the base of the cut. Those fish will get a good look at the bait. If your jig matches the size and color of what the fish are conditioned to eat, you will be setting a hook shortly.

If you try presenting your bait from any other direction, it will be impossible to fish the cut effectively. You might conclude the fish were not present or not hitting. Only a true visualization will allow you to "see" the structure and present a lure to the fish.

In some cases visualization may not involve creating mental images of structures on the bottom. For example, fish such as striped bass and salmon often inhabit mid-lake areas and relate to schools of forage fish or favored temperature zones. Visualizing in these situations requires picturing fish suspended in the water column somewhere between the bottom and the surface. A depthfinder is essential for pin-pointing schools of baitfish and suspended gamefish.

To review the visualization technique, start with a map clearly showing contour lines. Learn what the symbols in the legend represent, and identify the best fish-holding structures in the water. Then create a mental, 3-dimensional picture of each one. Locate fish at those structures with a depthfinder, or make an intelligent guess as to their location. Lastly, position your boat so that your lure presentation will reach the particular places fish are most likely to be.

When you fish with an accurate visualization of the underwater scene, you eliminate most of the random haphazards of angling. Visualization, particularly at first, takes time. The more you practice the technique, the more you realize it is time well spent.

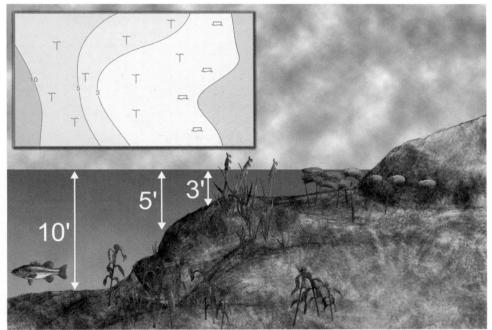

Figure 7.3 This diagram shows fish holding structure represented by contours bottom composition and vegetation.

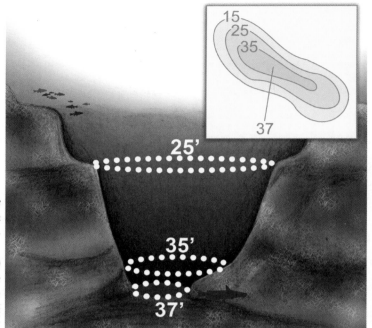

Hydrographic maps represent changes in elevation by concentric "circles."
Figure 7.4 *(right) shows what a hole looks like* **Figure 7.5** *(below) shows a hump.*

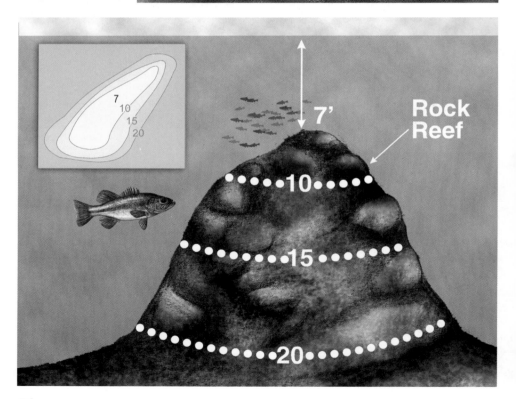

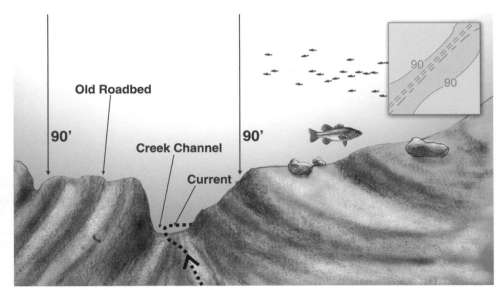

Figure 7.6 *An example of a submerged roadbed.*

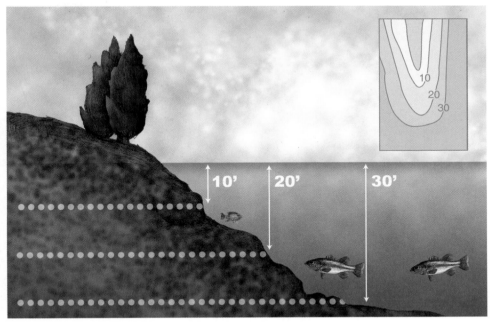

Figure 7.7 *An example of an underwater point and how fish are likely to relate to it.*

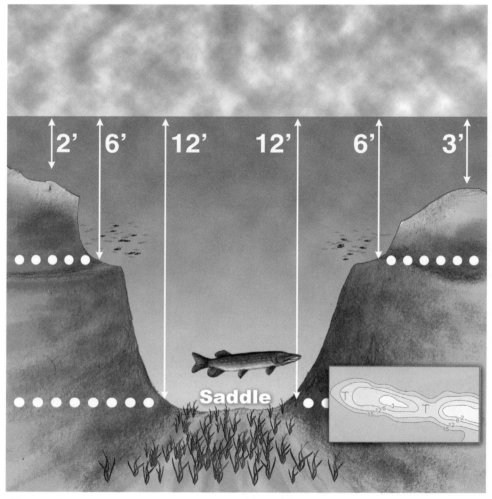

Figure 7.8 *Illustrated above is an example of a "saddle." The term "saddle" refers to an area of deep water that separates adjacent humps or reefs.*

Chapter 8
Locating Fish by Types of Water

The purely instinctive fish behaves exactly as nature demands, regardless of the type of water it inhabits. Trout go on a feeding frenzy during the height of a mayfly hatch whether they live in a cold Adirondack Mountain stream, swim the deep waters of north central Wisconsin's Fence Lake, or patrol the shallow, rock strewn Yellowstone River of Wyoming.

Although fish behavior is constant, each body of water they inhabit has its own personality. Anglers should recognize each water's individual peculiarities. Categorizing waters simplifies their analyses.

There are three basic types of inland waters: natural lakes and ponds, man-made reservoirs, and rivers. Natural lakes and reservoirs resemble each other closely. Rivers are more distinct in that they have a current or a constant flow of water.

If you look at two maps, one of an impounded reservoir and the other a natural lake, it may be difficult to detect any difference at first. The single most important distinction between the two is a dam at the lower end of the reservoir. (Some natural lakes have dams, but the effect is to stabilize water levels not create an entirely new body of water.) Lakes have natural boundaries, while the licensed agency that constructed the dam has defined the normal limits of a reservoir.

At least one river or creek supplies a reservoir with water. Most are fed by several inlets. Because of the variety of sources, reservoir water temperatures and clarities vary considerably more than a natural lake.

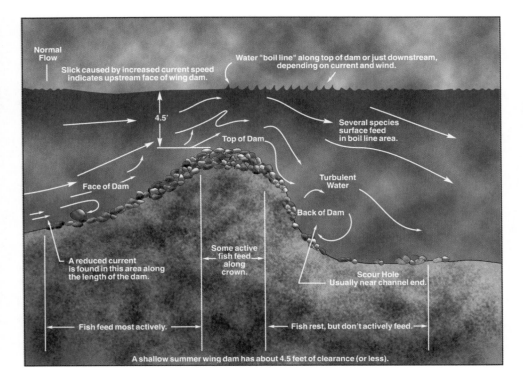

Let's assume you are fishing a reservoir. Your target species is white bass. Your buddy called yesterday and said, "The whites are hitting like crazy in the main lake off the old river channel. You better get down there as soon as you can."

Unfortunately, the very next day, you have not caught one white bass in three hours of plugging the old river channel. Upon reflection, you realize the water is crystal clear which means bass are very deep--too deep for you to effectively present a lure.

Where could you find less clear water and possibly a school of bass shallow enough to catch? Look at the map. Last night it rained. The reservoir's feeder creeks will bring silt with their normal flow. Those coves that have running water are going to get cloudy before the main lake. Fire up your motor and follow the map to the closest cove--a much more likely bass location than where you are presently fishing.

Another example of finding a fish-producing current in a reservoir is during the spawning runs of certain types of bass and the walleye. These species need moving water to stir their reproductive activities and produce the next generation. A good fishing map will show you these locations.

In a natural lake, where current is negligible, a map will still point out if water is moving and, therefore, attracting fish. Narrows or constricted areas often have current flow that attracts both forage and gamefish. If you know the direction of the wind, simply orient your map and you will see where the wind is stacking up against an island or shore. If that shore is a soft, erodible bank, it will also have the cloudiest water--another fish attractor.

Unless extensive clearing was done prior to the erection of a dam, reservoir water floods a host of potential fish structure. Old roadbeds, buildings or foundations, riprapping, creek channels, old ponds and lakes, timber, old bridges and towns are found on the bottoms of reservoirs. Each of these features is a potential fishing bonanza. Each is clearly marked on a fishing map.

Natural lakes have similar structural fish habitat--most are not man-made, however. Underwater humps, islands, weedbeds, rock piles, reefs, drop-offs, points, gravel and mud flats adjacent to deep water attract fish. You need a contour map to find most of these, too.

Fishing a river is different than a lake or reservoir. Fish behave the same no matter where you happen to be fishing, but in a river your strategy will be different from a lake or reservoir. If you can find a contour map of a river, that's great, but a river map will be of immense help to you, even if that map shows no underwater depths.

The rule, "always fish structure," applies in a river as in other bodies of water. Structure in a river does not necessarily resemble lake structure. In a reservoir, an old, flooded-over bridge supplies fish-holding cover. Bridges over a stream or river provide cover, not the entire bridge, of course, just the underwater pilings and support system.

A sharp turn in a submerged creek channel is a reservoir hot spot. A sharp turn in a river is a great spot to fish, too.

A hump in a natural lake serves as a sanctuary for moving fish. A boulder in a river's current serves the exact same function.

Fish relate to deep water, and in particular, to objects in deep water. Find a deep hole in a river, particularly one with fallen trees or other cover, and you have found preferred fish habitat.

These examples are the similarities between rivers, lakes and

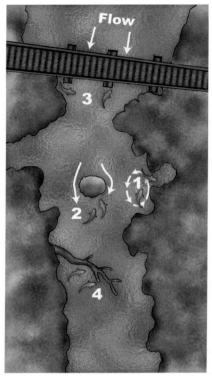

reservoirs. Now you need to develop a strategy for the peculiarities of rivers.

Although fly fishermen can ply their skills on any body of water, the sport was born on a river. Rivers and streams seem the natural setting for the long rod, heavy line fly caster.

River water constantly moves. Feeding fish face upstream into current, waiting for edibles to drift to them. Presentation of a fly, lure or bait upstream will be carried by the current downstream in front of fish.

River fish position themselves at strategic places to feed. A hungry fish will establish territory in slack water adjacent to current. The drawing to the left illustrates four such slack water feeding areas.

The first is the calm water of an eddy. The second is immediately behind a large, center-current boulder. The third is below the bridge's support columns in mid-current. The fourth is on the downstream side of a log.

Normally, anglers would cast upstream beyond the fish's holding points and retrieve their offering downstream.

What kind of map can you use to find places like these? Those rivers that serve as major shipping lanes, such as the Mississippi, Ohio, Hudson, St. Lawrence and Missouri, are mapped for navigation. Various types of charts are available for these large rivers.

The detail of county maps, which include everything from major rivers to the tiniest brook, have angler applications. These maps show bridge crossings, stretches where a stream runs close to a road, and some may even show public fishing areas. County maps are available from several state agencies and the offices of county or parish engineers.

The illustration pictured here shows a river crossed by two bridges **(#1)**. Two sharp turns in the stream **(#2)** indicate the probability of deep holes on the outside bend and a sand or gravel flat on the inside. At the middle of the map, you find a small island **(#3)** to divert current and serve as an ambush point for feeding fish. Even a county road map--not designed for anglers--is of immense help in fishing a river.

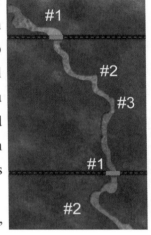

Shore fishermen, whether they fish rivers, ponds, lakes, reservoirs, dam tailwaters or even coastal estuaries and shorelines will find county maps helpful in locating the most convenient route to their favorite haunt as well as potential fish-laden waters.

Maps also locate public fishing piers, ponds in public parks, streams and creeks, levees, dikes, breakwaters, culverts, and access points. A shore angler can take advantage of all of these.

The saltwater shore angler uses maps to find a number of potentially good fishing areas. They should mark the following on their map: a tidal flat within casting distance that is close to deep water, rock points that jut into deep water, narrow gaps that ebb and flow during tidal changes, and deep water adjacent to the shore. Estuary anglers look for these same features as well as indentations in the shore, a river or stream delta, and high and low tide marks.

In the north country where lakes, reservoirs and even some rivers freeze solidly during winter, maps will provide directions to the right places to drill holes through the ice. The process of locating fish with a map is really no different on the ice than it was prior to the freeze. You will use your map, a compass and position lines. Since you can not see into the water directly, a portable depthfinder will tell you the depth and what kind of structure you are on.

When the ice reaches sufficient strength to hold a motor vehicle, an odometer can register distance according to the scale of the map. Measure the space from a road's end to the weedline or reef you intend to fish, and drive the appropriate distance and direction. Not even frozen water will deter the map-user from catching fish.

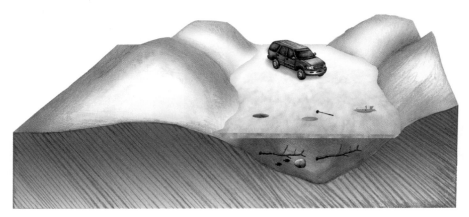

Figure 8.1 *Fishing maps are a valuable tool for the ice angler. Finding fish-holding structure under the ice is considerably easier with a map.*

Chapter 9
Navigation on the Water

F ishing maps are great tools for finding fish, but like most maps they are invaluable for getting from one place to another. Locating harbors, marinas, parks and boat landings is the most common use of fishing maps.

If you fish large, open waters, you need a map to find fishable locations and safely return to the boat landing. The last thing anyone needs is to get lost.

Finding An Underwater Hot Spot With Map & Compass

To navigate across water, you need a map and a compass. Any compass will work, but an orienteering compass--one that has a transparent base and a ruler will make your job much easier. The compass ruler measures the map's scale and lets you determine real-world distances. The transparent base lets you read through the compass on a map.

A compass needle does not always point directly north. Instead it aligns with a point close to true north called magnetic north--a condition created by the earth's magnetic fields. The difference between true north and magnetic north is called declination or compass variation. The compass rose on a map indicates the amount of declination or variation. It is important to remember that declination varies from area to area, so be sure to check for the local variation. The compass user should compensate his readings accordingly. Another caution: a compass is adversely affected by certain metals. Make sure your readings are taken at a safe distance from metallic objects.

STEP ONE: Orient the map. Start the process by letting the compass's magnetic needle point north.

Once you know where north is, open your map. A directional arrow or compass rose is printed on the map. Lay the map down on a flat surface and turn it until its north arrow agrees with the north arrow on your orienteering compass or boat compass.

Now that you have everything facing the right direction, north, look around to familiarize yourself with the shore and water shown on the map. When what you see agrees with the map, go to the next step.

STEP TWO: Measure distance. How far is it from your present position to the place you wish to travel? If there is a rock reef on the far end of the lake that you heard was a smallmouth bass hot spot, use the map's scale and the compass ruler to determine the exact distance.

You find the reef to be 2 miles southwest of your position. If your boat speed is 30 miles per hour, you need 4 minutes of travel time to get to the reef.

STEP THREE: Find the course or direction of travel. A compass is a magnetic needle that rotates around a 360-degree dial. The needle, when free to revolve, always points north. Place your compass on the properly oriented map (step1) so that both point north. Now, keeping the needle facing north, twist the base (not the dial) of the compass so the direction arrow points to the rock reef. Look along the direction arrow back to the dial. Where the line intersects the dial is the direction of travel to the destination.

STEP FOUR: Sighting a landmark (step 4). You are ready to lift the compass from the map and visually determine the precise direction of travel. With the compass in your hand, allow the needle to point north. Holding the dial northward, twist the base so that the direction of travel agrees with the course determined in step 3. Look in that direction and pick out the most prominent landmark such as a building, tall tree, oil well, or water tower. You will use that mark to navigate.

STEP FIVE: Arriving at your destination. Start your motor and, at a speed of 30 miles per hour, travel four minutes toward the pre-determined landmark. That's all you need to do to find the rock reef. When you get in the general area, use a depthfinder to make sure you are on the smallmouth haven.

Once you find the reef, mark its exact location for future reference and to make sure you do not float or drift off this important piece of structure. A common technique for marking a spot is throwing out marker buoys.

Another less obvious method of marking a spot is using position

Figure 9.1 *Dead reckoning navigating by referencing a prominent and distinct feature on the shoreline.*

lines.

When you are fishing a hot piece of structure and you know you want to return, mark the spot by doing the following:

• Locate some prominent and permanent feature on the water or shore like a brightly painted house, the tallest tree or a navigation buoy (see figure 9.1).

• Find another marker further up the shore and align them one behind the other.

• Draw a mental line from those features to your location. Turn 90 degrees, find two other prominent objects and draw a second line

Figure 9.2 *If an angler wants to return to a specific fishing spot he or she can locate two landmarks and draw "sight lines" to each one. The intersection of these two lines is the where the fishing spot is and can then be marked on a map.*

from them to your position. The intersection of these two lines pinpoints the reef.

The next time you want to fish that spot, travel along one of your lines and stop when you cross the other. The process is simple. To help you remember your prominent markers, make note of them on your map. You may even draw those lines on the map, assuring you'll find the exact spot again on your next trip.

Although the following chapter will present the latest technologies in navigation, knowing the simple use of a compass and map is fun, useful, and will reward you with bigger catches of fish, than if you go out completely "blind."

Chapter 10
Electronic Navigation

A nglers today can have an eagle's eye view of the waters they fish. Because of the bird's keen eyesight and ability to fly at great heights, the eagle can fly directly to any fish-holding spot it wishes. Anglers can approximate the eagle's navigational and fish-finding abilities, if they own the technology. Two such technologies are LORAN-C (LOng RAnge Navigation System) and GPS (Global Positioning System).

Before beginning a discussion of these sophisticated systems, you need to understand a few basic concepts about mapping and navigation. LORAN-C is an older (considered obsolete by some and planned to be disabled in the coming years) technology that uses a series of land-based radio transmitters. LORAN'S availability is limited by the location of the transmitters, and its accuracy is degraded by variables such as atmospheric conditions. GPS is a more recent technology that uses satellite based transmitters. Its worldwide availability and high level of accuracy have resulted in numerous civilian applications in addition to its original military function.

A series of imaginary grid lines known as latitude and longitude divide the planet. These lines are reference points. Latitude lines (circles running parallel to the equator) and longitude lines (circles running from pole to pole) grid the earth. Each line has been given a number. The equator is numbered zero. The longitudinal line numbered zero runs through Greenwich, England, and is known as the Greenwich or Prime Meridian.

The basic unit of measurement for the earth's imaginary grid is degrees, since the longitude and latitude lines are circles and a circle has 360 degrees. Degrees are made up of sub-units called minutes; minutes are made up of smaller units known as seconds.

Grid lines, other than the two zero lines, number consecutively as you travel from the standard or zero line. Longitude numbers range from 0 to 180, latitude from 0 to 90. Latitude lines above the equator are given a north designation; those below a south. Longitude lines are given east or west designations relative to the Prime Meridian.

You can find any place on the earth, including your favorite fishing spot, if you know its longitude and latitude numbers. A set of latitude and longitude numbers is referred to as a coordinate. For example, to find Niagara Reef in the Western Basin of Lake Erie look for the intersection of north latitude 41 degrees, 39 minutes, 52 seconds and west longitude 82 degrees, 58 minutes, 27 seconds. In other words, the reef is 41+ degrees north of the Equator and 82+ degrees west of the Greenwich line.

Why is this information useful to the average angler? Fishing Hot Spots fishing maps, for example, include latitude and longitude coordinates so that anglers can navigate with numerical accuracy. These maps go an astronomical step further--their coordinates are from the latest satellite navigation system, GPS. Global Positioning System is a product of the United States Department of Defense. Basically, GPS determines an exact latitude and longitude location by way of a system of satellites beaming signals to earth. Actually there are 21 GPS transmitting satellites orbiting the earth. Each GPS orbiter broadcasts highly accurate positioning data and times.

Similar to sonar (discussed more extensively in Chapter 6), a GPS receiver picks up signals from the satellites, measures the signal's travel time, and calculates the distance between the receiver and each selected satellite. Readings from four satellites are required to get an accurate 3-dimensional (latitude, longitude and altitude) position. The receiving device then translates this data and calculates a precise location. The latitude and longitude coordinates, as well as the altitude at the point of reception, are displayed. The electronic instrument tells you exactly where you are.

A common GPS application for anglers is traveling easily and directly from one part of a large body of water to another. Let's go back to Lake Erie's Western Basin for a moment. Say you are fishing off Airport Reef (N 41^0, 35', 59" & W 82^0, 39', 57") and you want to move to Mill Point Reef (41^0, 44', 35" & W 82^0, 36', 20"). To facilitate your move, enter your present position, then enter the latitude/longitude coordinates of Mill Point Reef. Depending on the type of GPS unit you have, you can press the GO TO function and the GPS screen will display the direction to travel, the time it will take, and a map for you to follow on it's plotter screen. Some units even whistle when you arrive at your destination!

Other angler uses for GPS include precise location and bait presentation. That's another way of saying marking fish-holding cover and trolling a plug effectively.

What if you find a submerged brush pile loaded with foot-long,

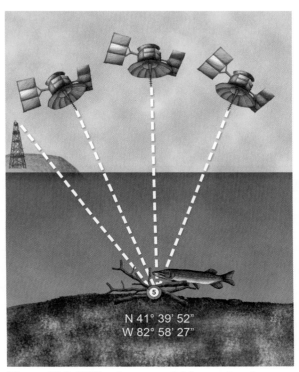

N 41° 39' 52"
W 82° 58' 27"

Figure 10.1 GPS units are useful for storing the coordinates of prime fishing spots.

hungry crappie. You sure want to mark that spot on your fishing map with a big red X. When you have to leave the spot and want to return later, you could throw out a marker buoy. With that visible marker, however, everyone else on the lake knows your spot too.

With a GPS unit you can create an invisible, electronic marker that allows you to return to the exact brush pile. All you do is push a button on the GPS unit and it automatically records the position's coordinates. Later, when you want to catch a bucketful of crappie, you enter the coordinates for the brush pile and the GPS unit pinpoints the site and guides you to it.

You can do the same thing when you want to troll an irregularly shaped weedline or breakline. Just enter a series of coordinates (also called waypoints) at strategic intervals along your trolling route, and use your GPS unit to keep you on track.

GPS devices are available to anglers as portable hand-held models, or as units that are mounted on the boat either as GPS only or combined with a depthfinder. Prices of GPS receivers vary tremendously according to features, precision and quality. Advancing technologies and market place competition continue to affect consumer costs.

Chapter 11
Digital Fishing Maps

In today's increasingly digital world and with the advancement of technology, digital fishing maps are available for your GPS and chartplotter electronics. Manufacturers like Lowrance® provide digital fishing maps, either pre-loaded on their electronic units or available for purchase as an add-on chip, containing all the information available on Fishing Hot Spots® maps. On your units screen you can see a quality fishing map and access the fishing information you need to be successful.

Of course, as with any technology item, there is a learning curve and a period of adjustment that is needed to fully understand and begin using the tools to their fullest. Rest assured that it will be time well spent.

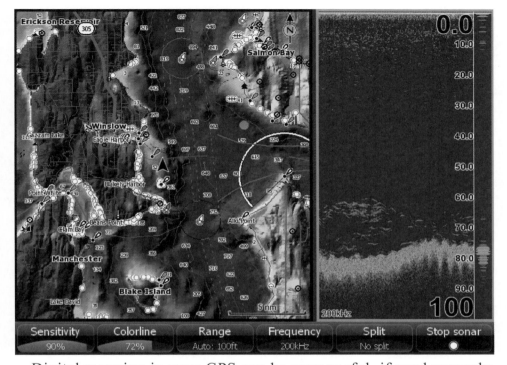

Sensitivity	Colorline	Range	Frequency	Split	Stop sonar
90%	72%	Auto: 100ft	200kHz	No split	●

Digital mapping in your GPS can be very useful, if used properly. Most successful anglers use their digital mapping unit in a split-screen mode. This divides the display into two halves, with one half containing the map from the chip and the other half showing the sonar reading. By using your electronics in this manner you are able to see, not only what is directly under your boat but, what the depth changes are that you're approaching. This allows you to fish more effectively because you can see where you need to cast and how to present your bait based on the lake bottom.

Say you're out fishing and you find active fish holding on a small hump in the middle of the lake; with your GPS unit containing a digital map you can save GPS coordinate of the hump which will be displayed on the map. This will allow you to return to the stop another time and, with the visual aid of the digital map, mark the same location on your paper map for further study back at camp.

Using electronic and paper maps together is the one-two punch in location fishing. Top pros will use their paper map to plan their day and develop a strategy, before they even get on the water. Taking their map with them they will use it to guide themselves to high-potential areas and switch over to their electronics, set in split-screen mode, to optimize their fishing time. At days end, they return to their paper map, mark it up with the day's events and make notes to prepare themselves for the next day.

Another key advantage to incorporating digital mapping into your electronics is in navigation assistance. The map will show you where you've been, where you need to go and provide you with hazards and landmarks to watch, or watch out, for. No more guessing which side of an island is safe passage, it's displayed for you.

Digital maps are not the only thing that electronics can provide while on the water. Included with all Fishing Hot Spots, Inc. digital map offerings is the where-to/how-to fishing information that Fishing Hot Spots is known for. Pre-determined fishing locations are provided, along with suggestions on the best technique, bait and presentation to use at the spot.

Many manufacturers also include a large amount of points of interest (POI's) that are of interest to anglers and boaters alike. Marina locations, along with the services offered for each are often available; as are restaurants and lodging facilities to name just a few information types. If you're on the water and its lunchtime, just search for the nearest place that serves food and the unit will tell you where it is.

The added convenience and accessibility of information with the digital mapping options available for GPS/chartplotter devices is a time saver and allows you to fish more efficiently.

Properly incorporating digital maps and GPS into your fishing tools will payoff in the end. From ease of use, to comprehensive information, today's electronics offer anglers tremendous options and versatility in improving their fishing success. Of course, with all the utility and advancement of electronic units, you still can't spread them out on the table and see what happened on an entire lake at one glance, for this you still need a paper map.

Afterword

Map makers provide highly detailed descriptions of the surface and subsurface features of the finest fishing waters in North America. Their maps make the process of finding fish easier than ever before. It is up to you, the angler, to take full advantage of these remarkable products.

Reading and interpreting a fishing map will allow you to catch fish with consistency you never thought possible. So grab your rod and reel, Catch Fish with MAPS, a GPS unit and the fishing map of your favorite lake and get on the water with greater success.

A Look Ahead

The only thing that is certain and unchangeable is change itself. This certainly holds true for fishing maps. In this section of a previous version of this book it was suggested that digital lake maps and underwater cameras may be developed *someday*. That day has come and now all anglers have the advantage of these technologies.

The future of fishing maps may have more to do with how anglers get their maps as opposed to what they do with them. Perhaps someone is working on delivering fishing maps and information wirelessly to your phone, PDA or personal navigation device.

Perhaps someone else is working on an internet application that allows you to go online to view fishing maps, mark them up, and print them for your use; or download them, one at a time, to your electronic mapping unit.

Maybe the future will hold an all new technology where a single sheet of plastic-like material can be the wireless receiver for your fishing map. Just pull it out of your pocket, unfold it and the map of where you're at appears.

Technology is advancing at a remarkable rate, and so is the fishing map. Today's maps are more accurate than ever before and there is certain to be innovations in the years to come. We'll just have to wait and see what those are so we can continue to Catch more Fish With Maps.

Acknowledgements

Publication of this book would not have been possible without the assistance and contributions of many organizations and individuals. Special thanks are extended to the following for their involvement and contributions toward this book's content and images:

Lowrance Electronics
Magellan Electronics
Ann M. Smith
Mark C. Martin
Tom Richards
National Oceanic and Atmospheric Association
United States Geological Survey
United States Army Corps. of Engineers
Tennessee Valley Authority

Cover Design:
Christopher Rogers – Photography and Design
Lowrance Electronics – Photography

Production Staff:
Illustrations, Layout and Design: Christopher Rogers
Editor: Steve Swierczynski

Glossary

Contour Interval:	The change in depth or elevation represented by adjacent contour lines.
Coordinate:	The intersection of longitudinal and latitudinal lines to locate a specific point on a map.
Cone Angle:	The size (expressed in degrees) of the funnel-shaped signal pattern produced by a depthfinder's transducer.
CRT:	Cathode Ray Tube, a particular type of depthfinder display. Also referred to as video.
Datum:	Indicates how a map is referenced to its actual position within the world.
Dead Reckoning:	The form of navigation using line of sight (usually refers to using no electronic or direction-finding device).
Drop-off:	A marked increase in the rate of depth change.

Access: An area that provides a place to get on or near the water. Typically a boat landing, but may also include fishing piers, canoe portages and road right-of-ways.

Aquatic Vegetation: Plants that grow in or very near the water. There are three major classifications:
> *Submergent* – Plants commonly found growing beneath the surface. (pondweeds, coontail, milfoil)
> *Floating* – Plants or portions of plants that float on the water's surface. (lily pads, water shield, duckweed)
> *Emergent* – Rooted vegetation commonly found in shallow water or along lake or river margins. Much of the plant stands out of the water. (tule, bulrush, pickerel weed)

Bathymetry: The bottom, elevation structure of a lake or waterway *(see also Contour Interval)*

Brackish: A mixture of salt and freshwater.

Bottom Composition: Bottom types in a body of water, typically rock, sand, gravel, cobble, bedrock, silt, muck, or marl.

Breakline: An area where there is a definite change in depth, bottom composition, temperature or clarity.

Buoy: A cone or cylindrical marker in the water designating channels, harbor entrances, obstructions and restrictions.

Contour Lines: Lines that indicate the shape and range of a specific depth or elevation on hydrographic and topographic maps.

Edge: The border fringe of any fish-holding habitat – weeds, wood, brush, rock, etc. A good place to fish.

Fertility: The nutrient level of water that dictates its biological productivity.

Fish Attractor: Structures designed to concentrate fish or provide cover. Often man-made, common types include brush piles, tire reefs, Christmas tree piles, and log cribs.

Fishery: The collective group of fish that inhabit a lake.

Flasher: A type of depthfinder display most often using a neon light that flashes at calibrated intervals depending on depth.

Forage Fish: Species consumed by gamefish. Also called baitfish. Common types include shad, smelt, various minnows and juvenile panfish.

GPS: An abbreviation for Global Positioning System. A satellite-based navigation system first developed by the military but now used by fishermen and boaters.

Gamefish: The group of prized fish sought by anglers. Includes bass, pike, trout and salmon.

Habitat: An area to which fish relate and can often be found. Usually associated with some form of structure.

Hump: A structure that rises above the lake bottom surrounded by deeper water. Also called a submerged island.

Hydrographic Map: A map or chart of an aquatic area that usually depicts various bottom features and depths.

Impoundment: A reservoir or man-made lake created when a dam is built across a stream.

Latitude: The imaginary map grid lines that circle the earth and run parallel to the Equator.

LCD: Liquid Crystal Display. A type of depthfinder display screen commonly used by anglers.

Legend: The map component that defines the symbols used to represent various land and water features shown on a map. Sometimes called a map key.

Longitude: The imaginary map grid lines that run perpendicular to the Equator and pass through the North and South poles.

LORAN-C: An electronic navigation system that uses a series of land-based radio transmitters.

Magnetic North: North as indicated by a compass needle. Magnetic north varies from true north by the amount of variation (declination) caused by the earth's magnetic fields.

Marker Buoy: A variety of floats, bottles and jugs used by anglers to mark a spot, outline structure, or to return to a precise location.

Migration Route: Routes taken by gamefish as they move from one area to another.

Navigational Aids: Any buoy, daymark, light or beacon placed in or near the water to provide navigational information.

Panfish: A group of relatively small, usually edible, abundant fish sought by anglers that includes perch, bluegill, rock bass, crappie, sunfish and bullhead.

Pattern: The specific and predicted behaviors of fish during a particular period of time.

Projection: A method for displaying the surface of a sphere, the Earth, on a flat paper.

Riprap: Rock or broken concrete placed along a shoreline or channel bank to prevent erosion or create breakwaters.

Scale: The proportional units of measurement used to correlate actual distance with map distance.

Structure: Natural or man-made feature of a fish's environment above or below the water line that most species relate to for food, protection and comfort.

Stratify: The characteristic of a lake to develop distinct temperature layers.

Suspended: The position of fish not closely related to bottom or structure.

Symbol: A graphic, image or styled line on a map or chart used to represent a particular, real-world feature.

Tailwaters: The part of a river immediately below a dam, usually characterized by swift, turbulent flow and a hard bottom.

Thermocline: A layer of well-oxygenated lake water that displays a rapid drop in temperature.

Topographic: A map type depicting surface elevation and other land characteristics.

Visualization: The process of mentally creating a three-dimensional image of a fish's world.

Waypoints: A series of latitude/longitude or other coordinates that define a route of travel.